VEGAN BRISTOL

BEN McCABE & HELENA MURPHY

VEGAN BRISTOL

Ben McCabe and Helena Murphy

Published by Bristol Books, 2024

Bristol Books CIC, The Courtyard, Wraxall,
Wraxall Hill, Bristol, BS48 1NA
www.bristolbooks.org

ISBN: 9781909446410

Copyright © Ben McCabe and Helena Murphy

Designed and typeset by Ben McCabe
Photography by Helena Murphy

Ben McCabe and Helena Murphy have asserted their rights under the Copyright, Designs and Patents Act of 1988 to be identified as the authors of this work.

All rights reserved. This book may not be reproduced or transmitted in any form or in any means without the prior written consent of the publisher, except by a reviewer who wishes to quote brief passages in connection with a review written in a newspaper or magazine or broadcast on television, radio or on the internet.

To request permission to use any part of this book, write to the publisher addressed "Permissions Coordinator" at the following email address: ben@keskorra.co. A CIP record for this book is available from the British Library.

This product is made of material from well-managed, FSC®–certified forests and other controlled sources.

Supported by Essential Trading Co-operative.

A LOVE LETTER

Bristol is a truly remarkable city when it comes to food. When we moved from London to Bristol in 2020 to be closer to our South West roots, we were worried we might struggle to find the same diversity of plant-based options that we had at our fingertips while living in the capital.

We needn't have worried. From pop-ups and speciality delis to vegan-only takeaways and fine dining establishments offering beautifully curated, veg-first dishes, we found ourselves spoiled for choice. Fast forward to 2024 and options have proliferated as venues across the city have leant into the insatiable demand from Bristolians for ethical yet still delicious food options. It's genuinely never been a better time to be vegan in Bristol.

Despite this, the past few years have been truly tough for hospitality businesses: first the Covid-19 pandemic forced closures across the board, followed by a painfully slow return of customers as it ended. No sooner had normality returned when the cost of living crisis saw spiralling energy bills and supply costs, which reduced the spare cash people have to spend. As two people who love to eat and love to create, we wanted to celebrate and draw attention to the vibrancy and resilience of Bristol's diverse, delicious vegan food scene.

Not all of the establishments listed in the book are 100% vegan, but all are 100% tasty. We believe in celebrating inclusivity and flexibility, recognising the places who have put just as much thought and time into their plant-based options as everything else on their menu. We hope you enjoy eating your way around the city as much as we have while making this book!

Helena and Ben

CONTENTS

17
16
10
18
STOKES CROFT
COTHAM
CABOT CIRCUS
09
07
THE CENTRE
18
CASTLE PARK
19
31
05
15
01
08
COLLEGE GREEN
03
04
QUEEN SQUARE
02
A
06
TEMPLE MEADS
14
B
WHARF
12
11
13
10
C

CENTRAL BRISTOL

BS1

01

NUTMEG STREET FOOD

Elevated dishes inspired by Indian street market food

FLEXITARIAN

23-25 St Augustine's Parade, BS1 4UL

nutmegstreetkitchen.com

From the team behind Nutmeg Clifton, Nadu [p56] and Kal Dosa [p122], Nutmeg Street Kitchen was conceived as a way to bring a slice of India's vibrant street markets to the heart of central Bristol.

Walking into Nutmeg Street Kitchen is a balm for the soul; pops of baby pink and splashes of emerald green adorn the walls, alongside rattan and wicker accents and colourful artwork inspired by traditional Indian matchbox designs.

The menu has been created with care by Shishir Sinha, the chef behind Benares, a Michelin-starred Indian restaurant in Mayfair and other fine-dining institutions.

Across the menu, you can really sense the dedication and vision that has gone into making Nutmeg into something truly special, with a selection of dishes that are both warmingly comforting and offer a refreshing take on familiar flavours.

It says something when an omnivorous restaurant puts just as much love and attention into their plant-based dishes as the rest of their menu and – while small – Nutmeg's vegan options are excellent. The stand-out dish is the *mirchi aur kumbhi*, an Indian and Italian inspired recipe made of vegan cheese and nutmeg-flavoured portobello mushrooms and capsicum.

Outside of this, you really can't go wrong by mixing and matching the sides, starters and mains, from the delectable *pindi chole* and *jeera aloo* to the moreish *bhindi masala* and *beguner birinchi*.

It's advisable to book ahead from Thursday through to Sunday as this city centre venue quickly gets packed out – and with good reason. Even in a city with countless Indian restaurants, Nutmeg Street Kitchen stands out as something a bit different: an effortlessly classy space serving unfailingly delicious food.

YOU MUST TRY...

Mirchi aur Kumbhi
Pindi Chole
Beguner Birinchi

EAT IN DELIVERY

NANDI
SAFETY MATCHES

02

PASTAN

Wholly plant-based pasta dishes served with a Hispanic twist

VEGAN

53 Prince Street, BS1 4QH

pastan.co.uk

When you think 'vegan', creamy, cheesy bowls of gorgeously presented fresh pasta aren't necessarily the first thing to come to mind. Cue Pastan: a Hispanic-influenced Italian on a mission to change how we all think about vegan pasta.

With locations in Bristol, Brighton, London and now Barcelona, Pastan's menu boasts a collection of year-round items inspired by both classic Italian dishes – such as *cacio e pepe* – as well as changing seasonal creations, many of which offer a Spanish culinary twist, like the spicy, tomato-infused *Formentera* made with a fiery 'Nduja paste.

Dishes to try include the monster-sized *shiitake caesar salad* – filled with pulled shiitake mushrooms, deep fried gnocchi, cashew parmesan and 'chicken' nuggets – as well as comfort signatures like their plant-based take on *mac & cheese* with crispy onions and toasted breadcrumbs.

With a generous menu offering a wide gamut of flavour – from fresh and zesty to rich and tomatoey – it's a the kind of meal where you'll regret not getting an extra dish for the table to share.

While the pasta is definitely the hero of the story, their take on tapas classic *pan con tomate* is a great way to start off your meal – and don't forget to save room for the hands-down genius *mini biscoff doughnuts*: tiny pillows of fluffy delight, filled with hot biscoff sauce.

With its pops of pastel pink and deep green paint and its leafy plant-life, Pastan feels welcoming, fun and modern; its city centre location makes it the perfect spot for a meal, whether you are grabbing a salad on a long lunch with co-workers or dining out with friends and family to celebrate a special occasion in the evening.

YOU MUST TRY...

Cacio e Pepe
Shiitake Caesar Salad
Mini Biscoff Doughnuts

EAT IN DELIVERY

RENATO'S

Detroit and New York pizza in a reopened Italian favourite

VEGETARAN • VEGAN

33 King Street, BS1 4DZ

renatosbristol.com

For many in the city, Renato's has long been a synonym for pre-theatre food and late night slices. Before it closed its doors during the pandemic, the previous incarnation – run by the children of the eponymous Renato – had been operating as an Italian restaurant since the 1980s (and more recently, as a pizzeria only), and played host to a huge array of celebrities and locals alike over the years.

The new incarnation is a collaboration between Left Handed Giant brewery and Pizza is Lovely; a tasteful restoration that aims to celebrate and retain many of the features that made the original so iconic.

The upstairs restaurant has been restored to its former glory (think dark wood, patterned carpet and wonky floors) and serves the Detroit-style pizza on a twice-proved foccacia base that Pizza Is Lovely first made its name with. Alongside this is a range of complementary seasonal sides, including *padrón peppers*, various salads and mouthwatering *oven roasted garlic potatoes.*

Accompanying this is a generous selection of Italian wines ranging from classics to more natural skin-contact varieties, as well as a curated cocktail selection (including an entire negroni menu!).

Downstairs has been retained as a bar for drinks and grab-and-go food, selling New York style pizza by the slice along with a wide selection of Left Handed Giant beers (many of them vegan); this includes an Italian-style pilsner brewed especially for the location as its house lager.

The ambition with Renato's is to use independent suppliers where possible and make as much as it can in-house – this includes making the delicious vegan 'honey' that adorns a number of its pizza options, as well as its plant-based cheeses.

While this new iteration of Renato's is certainly different to what went before, it is a tasteful modernisation of the original – and now the ideal place to grab a plant-based slice when you find yourself in the city centre. The upstairs menu might seem pricey on the face of it but don't be fooled: the pizzas are large (8" x 10"), deep-dish and lend themselves to sharing – ideally with a side of *cheesy garlic dough balls.*

EAT IN DELIVERY

04

THREE BROTHERS

American-style burgers and sides on a harbourside barge

FLEXITARIAN

Welsh Back, BS1 4SB

threebrothersburgers.co.uk

Docked at the end of the pub-laden King Street, Three Brothers has grown over the years beyond Spyglass – the cavernous vessel that still hosts its kitchen – and spilled out onto the quay beyond. The result is a generously-sized restaurant mirrored by its portion sizes: nothing is sold by halves here, with burgers bursting at the seams and generous sides to accompany them.

Just as the venue itself is split between land and water, so Three Brothers' menu is divided equally between plant-based and meat-based dishes – a legacy of one of its chefs going vegan and pushing for a more inclusive menu.

All of Three Brothers' vegan patties and strips are made in-house – either with grains and vegetables or homemade seitan (the former for its vegan 'beef'; the latter for its plant-based 'chicken'). Among the substantive burger options is their classic *smokey bro*, with smoked Applewood, BBQ relish & crispy onions, while their *chilli burger* is a sloppy cacophony of chilli, jalapeños and American-style cheese that is impossible not to make a complete mess with as you eat.

By comparison the sides menu is short but sweet, offering a selection of dirty fries, deep fried pickles and incredibly moreish seitan strips. To complement the food, Three Brothers serves a generous array of gluten-free and vegan beers and ciders, largely drawn from local breweries. Anyone heading there around the festive season can try their Christmas specials (which always come as copycat meat-free and meat versions).

The name isn't a nod to the restaurant's founders as some have speculated – one theory suggests that it refers to the three masts on the boat itself. Whatever the origins of the name, what is not in question is that Three Brothers does what it does well, and at a reasonable price for a city centre venue.

YOU MUST TRY...

'Chicken' Strips and Dip
Smokey Bro Burger

EAT IN DELIVERY

THREE BROTHERS BURGERS

THREE BROTHERS
BURGERS

DHAMAKA

Vibrant pan-Indian flavours served with care and attention

FLEXITARIAN

15 Clare Street, BS1 1XH

dhamakadining.co.uk

'Dhamaka' is a Hindi word meaning 'blast' or 'explosion' – an appropriate name for an establishment where everything is a riot of colour and taste. This is clear from the moment you step inside: brightly coloured murals and artwork adorn the walls and each chair is painted in a different primary colour. The window frames are bright orange. It is a chaotic yet vibrant vibe, one that perfectly reflects the vividness of the food on offer.

The menu itself takes inspiration from across the Indian subcontinent (and a whole section of Indo-Chinese street food dishes), resulting in a unique menu full of diverse flavours and styles.

While Dhamaka was originally conceived without vegan dining as a focus, the team has steadily introduced more options over the years as it realised there was a keen demand for it, driven by favourites such as the *cauliflower manchurian* – a gloriously sticky, moreish dish that you may end up fighting over if you only order one – and a *kofta curry* with a real kick to it, made with a coconut madras sauce and warming vegetable dumplings.

Inclusivity is an important part of what Dhamaka offers – as well as several dishes labelled gluten-free, the kitchen eschews nuts entirely, which is no mean feat considering their popularity in many Indian dishes. As well as a vegan-friendly beer and cocktail selection, their wine list is entirely vegan.

One thing to note is that they can make their *plain*, *garlic* and *peshwari* naans as vegan on request – just make sure you specify you want the vegan version when you place your order!

While you can purchase Dhamaka for delivery, it's definitely worth paying their restaurant a visit so you can enjoy the hustle and bustle of its bright, airy venue while being fed very well indeed.

YOU MUST TRY...

Cauliflower Manchurian
Vegetable Momos (Nepalese dumplings)
Pershwari Naan (ask for it vegan)

TAKEAWAY DELIVERY

Indian

06

SUYUAN

Meat-free Chinese retaurant with authentic home-cooked vibes

VEGETARIAN • VEGAN

Grove Avenue, Queen Square, BS1 4QY

suyuan.co.uk

If you're looking for what typically passes for Chinese food in the UK, then you won't find that at Suyuan. The menu is diverse and unapologetically faithful to its Asian origins, drawing its inspiration from the Zumiao Taoist temple in Foshan, China and making simple but nourishing vegetarian Chinese food.

Tucked away just off Queen Square, this unimposing restaurant often flies under the radar – but with a real variety of fresh flavours and authentic dishes, it is well worth making the time to visit.

Most of the dishes served have their roots in the Hainan cuisine of Southern China, along with a few plates inspired by North Chinese cooking. Notably, every dish is freshly prepared and can be made vegan – a rarity in the UK where many Chinese restaurants offer little more than a couple of token dishes that are 'accidentally vegan'.

While there is a liberal use of tofu – ubiquitous across much Asian cooking – Suyuan makes a real effort to make vegetables the star of the show, with many dishes featuring aubergine, mushrooms, broccoli and even taro as the main ingredient. Most of the menu is relatively mild with subtle flavours, although spice fiends will find a couple of dishes – including the *stir fried cauliflower* with a dry chilli and garlic sauce – that ramp up the spiciness.

If you do want to drink alcohol during your meal it is BYOB; however, Suyuan offers a wide selection of excellent speciality teas, which offer an ideal accompaniment to its food.

If you're looking for comfort eating and are in the mood to try something new, then Suyuan might be exactly what you're looking for: unpretentious, homely and generous portion sizes to boot.

EAT IN TAKEAWAY

07

EDNA'S KITCHEN

Vegetarian falafel kiosk on the edge of Castle Park

VEGETARIAN • VEGAN

Castle Park, Castle Street, BS1 3XD

ednas-kitchen.com

Israeli-born chef Edna Summerell lays claim to being the first person to bring homemade hummous to Bristol in the 1980s; whether this is strictly true or not, her falafel kiosk in Castle Park has long since become a vegetarian staple for visitors and Bristolians alike.

With a selection of vegetarian and vegan Middle Eastern and Mediterranean dishes with a focus on healthy, organic ingredients, Edna's is known for its pittas and wraps loaded with freshly made falafel, salad, pickles and tahini.

Alongside wraps, punters can choose from salads and deli items including *baba ganoush*, *gluten-free tabouleh* and, of course, Edna's famous *hummous*.

While the venue has no indoor seating, there are outdoor tables available, as well as seating further into Castle Park for those wanting some breathing space from the traffic climbing up Broad Weir.

YOU MUST TRY...

Falafel Pitta with hummous, salad, pickles and tahini

TAKEAWAY

OOWEE VEGAN

Super satisfying fast food with 100% plant-based credentials

VEGAN

65 Baldwin Street, BS1 1QZ • 54 Picton Street, BS6 5QA • 202 North Street, BS3 1JF

ooweevegan.com

Think burgers. Dirty fries. Milkshakes. Tenders. Mac and Cheese. Think of fast food in all its glory, then make it vegan. That's what you get with Oowee.

Founders Charlie and Verity first started slinging burgers from their Picton Street location in 2016. From the outset, Oowee was intended as a love letter to junk food, with a menu shaped to mirror some of the amazing fast food they'd tried over the years.

This ambition clearly resonated with Bristolians. After seeing queues down the street, they opened a second venue on North Street in Southville, with both venues serving a half-and-half meat and veggie menu.

When there was a widespread outcry following their decision to take their popular *sneaky clucker* – a vegan fried 'chicken' burger – off the menu, the team set to remaking their entire menu with plant based alternatives, eventually launching their first all-vegan diner on Baldwin Street in 2018.

Since then, Oowee Vegan has gone from strength to strength: both Baldwin St and Picton St are now fully vegan, proving there is considerable demand for their unique blend of fully vegan fast food done to a high standard.

As well as their now established range of classic burgers, fries and milkshakes, the Oowee team is constantly innovating with their menu: recent additions are *vegan shrimp* and *'fish' burgers*, as well as limited edition runs with unexpected delights such as *Korean BBQ burgers* and *Gochujang cauliflower bites.*

Increasingly, Oowee is partnering with smaller challenger brands such as Omni and Symplicity as well as putting local suppliers in the spotlight by using them in their short-term menu items – with the most popular options then finding a spot on their regular menu.

It would be easy to call the restaurant Bristol's plant-based answer to McDonalds. But it's far more than that. A beloved Bristolian institution, Oowee is firmly established as one of the first places people think of when seeking a plant-based fix to that fast food craving.

EAT IN TAKEAWAY DELIVERY

OOWEE

AHH TOOTS

A mountain of sweet treats housed in a fairy-tale Tudor building

FLEXITARIAN

17, Christmas Street, BS1 5BT

ahhtoots.co.uk

When I first read about Willy Wonka's chocolate factory, I imagined a culinary vista not unlike the front window of Ahh Toots. Piled high with as many kinds of cakes and sweet treats as you can imagine, it's the kind of display that can (and often does) cause people to stop and stare in awe, enticed by the sugary, sweet delights contained within its moody, timber-panelled interior.

Ahh Toots can be found at the foot of the Christmas Steps, in a Grade I-listed Tudor-fronted building rumoured to date back to the 13th Century. With its dimly-lit, wood-panelled interior and overflowing cake counter, you'd be forgiven for thinking that Ahh Toots had always been there, rather than being a recent replacement for the fish and chip shop that occupied the space for more than a century.

Instead, Ahh Toots' roots actually go back to St Nick's Market, where founder Tam first opened a café and started baking from it in 2014. After meeting their partner (and skilled pastry chef) Amy four years ago, the two decided to relocate Ahh Toots to a larger space where they could make and sell their products from the same venue, eventually moving to their current site on Christmas Street the day before the first Covid lockdown was announced.

While running as a takeaway and delivery business throughout the various lockdowns, Ahh Toots hit upon the idea of a 'window full of cakes' that has continued ever since.

Around thirty different options are available each day – with at least ten of those vegan – meaning that those used to picking from a meagre selection of plant-based options may find themselves with a severe case of indecisiveness while ordering.

As well as the vast array of cakes and sweet treats on display, there is a solid list of vegan drinks options – from coffees and teas to cordials, iced teas and soft drinks.

Breakfast items include vegan sausage sandwiches, granola and porridge, while sandwiches and salads are also served from noon (including a grab-and-go meal deal). For those looking for more extravagant creations, the team can even make vegan wedding and celebration cakes to order.

EAT IN TAKEAWAY DELIVERY

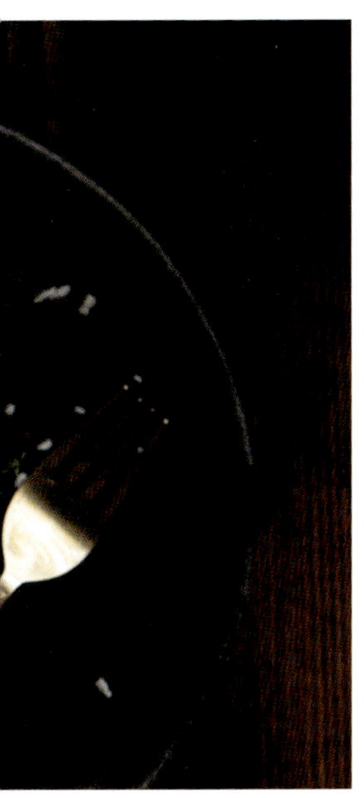

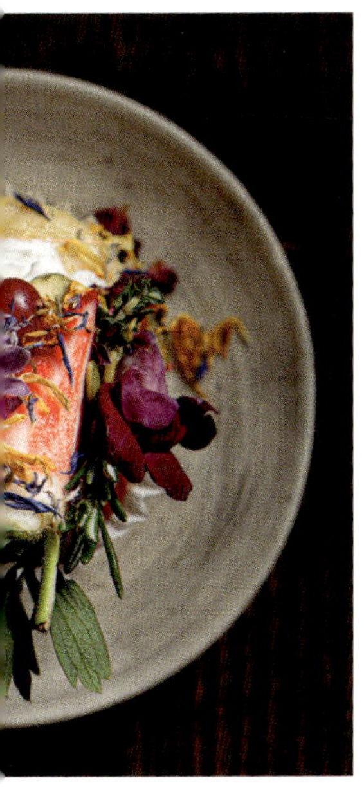

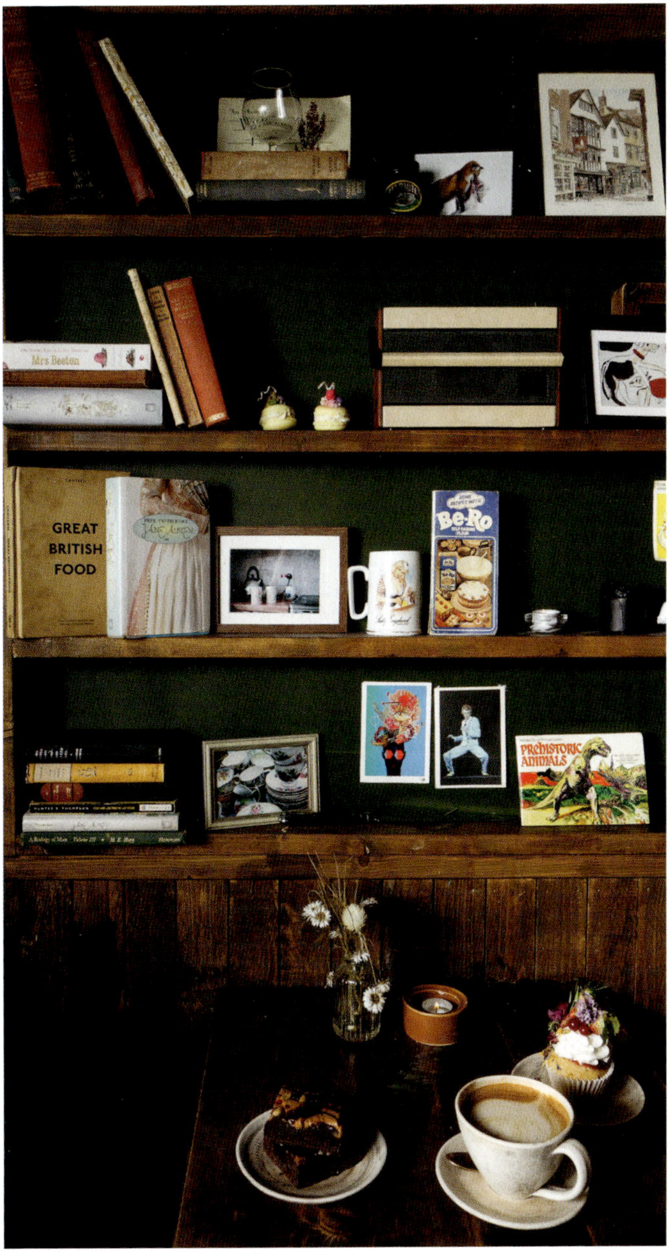
Mrs Beeton
GREAT
BRITISH
FOOD
Be-Ro
PREHISTORIC
ANIMALS

BIBLOS

A delicious collision of Caribbean and Middle Eastern flavours

FLEXITARIAN

Unit 6 Gaol Ferry Steps, BS1 6GW • 62A Stokes Croft, Bristol BS1 3QU

biblos.co.uk

Biblos began life as a restaurant serving classic Lebanese food in 2011, before adding in a Caribbean element after co-owner Will Clarke joined.

While this combination has raised a few eyebrows from customers unused to this unique combination, there's no doubt that it works – the spicy, fruity flavours of the Caribbean ingredients pair well with the fresh, earthy tastes of their Middle Eastern counterparts.

A key focus for the team has been staying authentic to its twin inspirations and making all of its key ingredients in-house at its Stokes Croft location, from its Caribbean-inspired marinades and delicious plant-based sauces to its falafel mix and vegan fried 'chicken'.

From day one Biblos' menu has been equal parts meat, veggie and vegan, with the aim to accommodate all kinds of dietary requirements.

Biblos is primarily known for its *wraps* and *salad boxes*, the former made with Khobez bread; both are available with several plant-based fillings including homemade falafel, vegan fried 'chicken', plantain and cauliflower tahini. These are typically paired with one of Biblos' homemade sauces – from yemen, chilli salsa and hot pepper to pineapple chilli jam and carob island sauce.

A diverse set of sides include *cauliflower tempura bites*, *hummus and flatbread* and *fried plantain*, while there are soft drinks, ciders, beers (including Red Stripe) and a selection of hot drinks.

While Biblos started out at a space in St Werburghs, it currently occupies two sites in Bristol: one in Stokes Croft and another in Whapping Wharf. As well as its restaurants, the Biblos team hits the road several times each year, serving its food at Glastonbury, Love Saves the Day and several other festivals.

YOU MUST TRY...

Cauliflower tahini wrap
Hummus and flatbread

EAT IN   DELIVERY

CHANGE IS NOW
www.florens.com
MAX. GROSS
TARE
MAX. CARGO
CU. CAP.
REBEL

BIBLOS

Elevated small plates in the heart of Wapping Wharf

FLEXITARIAN

Unit 9, Cargo 1, Gaol Ferry Steps, BS1 6WP

rootbristol.co.uk

Vegetable-led small plates restaurant Root can fairly be considered the obvious go-to for a slightly fancy date night in town (and that's even with it being situated in a Wapping Wharf shipping container). It's the kind of place where every plate sounds amazing but it might be a mystery as to exactly what will be coming out of the kitchen and how it might look on a plate. You can be sure that it will be delicious.

Root was opened in 2017 by Josh Eggleton and Luke Hasell – the pair have a prestigious history in the food industry under their belts. Eggleton is known for his transformation of The Pony and Trap in Chew Magna into one of a handful of UK pubs to hold a Michelin star, while chef Luke Hasell owns 500 acres of farm and runs an organic vegetable delivery service amongst his other ventures.

With a focus on sustainability and showcasing local ingredients, Root's seasonal small plates are designed to induce a dialogue between people and table. The team work fluidly and seasonally according to the produce available to them, sourcing from suppliers around Bristol, Bath and the Chew Valley.

Although there are a couple of meat or fish options on the menu, the majority of the menu features a constantly rotating menu of seasonal vegetables dressed up to the nines. For a taste of what to expect, picture a dish of *grilled hispi cabbage* served with a slathering of tahini, lemon, pickles and dukkah, or a plate of *roasted celeriac* dotted with apple, celery and walnuts.

Let the staff know you are vegan when you book and they'll bring over a menu showing how they can veganise many of the vegetarian options. Considering the fine dining vibes (this place has featured repeatedly in the Michelin guide) the prices are surprisingly reasonable for the quality you will find on the plate.

12

NEW CUT COFFEE

Colourful harbourside café with sublime coffee

VEGETARIAN • VEGAN

The Art Warehouse, Wapping Wharf, BS1 4RN

newcutcoffee.com

Housed in an iconic red Art Warehouse, New Cut Coffee is a coffeehouse staple on the waterfront of Bristol's Floating Harbour, a stone's through from the M Shed.

The small – but perfectly formed – space hosts a small outdoor seating area for catching the sun and enjoying the proximity to the water during the summer months, as well as a modern and minimal café space inside.

Adorned with plants, iconic horror movie posters and a vibey playlist, New Cut is a more than cosy nook to stop by for time out with a book or catching up with friends.

Working closely with local roasteries, New Cut serves both a bespoke espresso blend and a couple of single origin offerings, which are also available to buy for home brewing. As well as excelling at coffee, their salted caramel hot chocolate is a decadent delight and their delicious range of vegan pastries and cakes (sourced from 404 Bakes [p100]) is always a temptation – popular options include their *toasted banana bread* and *blueberry lattice pie*.

If you're in the mood for something a bit more filling, New Cut keeps a small rotation of plant-based sandwiches on offer with the likes of banana blossom, cajun cauliflower and sweetcorn chickpea patties available.

For those looking for something a bit different later in the day, they also offer a range of beers from local brewery Left Handed Giant.

EAT IN TAKEAWAY

NEW CUT
COFFEE
COFFEE
CAKES
SANDWICHES

13

SEVEN LUCKY GODS

Tokyo vibes and exciting flavours in a converted container

FLEXITARIAN

Cargo 2, Wapping Wharf, BS1 6UD

7luckygods.com

A small slice of neon-lit Tokyo in the heart of Bristol's harbourside, Seven Lucky Gods is Wapping Wharf's answer to the izakaya bars for which the Japanese capital is renowned. The concept of 'stay-drink-place' (the literal translation of izakaya) is immediately evident in the casual, freeform layout of the space: a large open plan kitchen is flanked by a long counter, along with indoor booths and a heated and covered outdoor seating area for those wanting to eat al fresco.

Part of the same group behind diverse offerings such as Flour and Ash pizzeria and Hyde & Co cocktail bar, Seven Lucky Gods is a love letter to Japanese food, with a three-part menu dedicated to sushi, charcoal grilled and fried dishes. Vegan options proliferate across each section, part of the team's stated intention to ensure that guests can enjoy the menu regardless of their diets.

It is hard to pick a stand-out dish among the excellent plant-based options, but the small portions and reasonable prices mean you can sample a wide range of tastes and flavours. As well as the *Nasu Den Maki* – panko aubergine and slaw maki rolls with miso vegan mayo – the *grilled broccoli*, *Sichuan-fried cauliflower* and *charred edamame* are all the kind of dishes you might be tempted to order multiple times in the same meal.

As well as serving Asahi on tap, Seven Lucky Gods offers a wide range of vegan-friendly drinks, including a couple of vegan wines, sake, kombucha and a variety of cocktails.

Packed into the containers of Cargo, Seven Lucky Gods makes good use of the space it has available; however, it does tend to get busy at times and booking ahead is often necessary.

YOU MUST TRY...

Nasu Den Maki
Grilled Broccoli Gomaae
Sichuan Fried Cauliower

EAT IN DELIVERY

SEVEN LUCKY GODS
XXX
七福神
BRISTOL · IZAKAYA

14

VEBURGER

Casual burger bar serving sustainable fast food

VEGAN

Unit 22 Museum Street, BS1 6ZA

veburger.co.uk

It's always worth taking a moment to appreciate when the basics are done well. Veburger strips the time-tested fast food approach back to its bare bones, focusing on serving the classics in an unfussy, unpretentious way. It has also managed to keep at bay the big price mark-up that a lot of plant-based food attracts.

Settled among the independent businesses at Wapping Wharf and serving out of a converted shipping container, Veburger offers an affordable collection of burgers, shakes and sides – with competitive pricing and lunch deals to encourage people to give plant-based fast food a go.

Veburger can be ordered for delivery or to eat at its harbourside location, where there is a small amount of indoor and outdoor seating available. Being right next to the M Shed, it is ideally situated for enjoying a quick bite while sat by the water on a sunny summer's day.

EAT IN TAKEAWAY DELIVERY

15

LEFT HANDED GIANT

Bustling three-storey Brewpub serving a veggie/vegan Neapolitan pizza menu

VEGETARIAN • VEGAN

Hawkins Lane, Finzels Reach, BS1 6EU

lhgbrewpub.com

Left Handed Giant's flagship Brewpub, located opposite Castle Park in the centre of the city, has always married great vegan beer options with quality plant-based food. Up until August 2023 it was home to wood-fired pizza specialists Mission Pizza, who rightly earned rave reviews for their creative, moreish veggie/vegan takes on Neapolitan pizza.

After that partnership ended, Left Handed Giant teamed up with the team behind Pizza is Lovely, who have taken over the on-site pizza oven to serve their own selection of Neapolitan pizzas, along with an intriguing set of sides – think truffle fire-roasted *new potatoes* or *meatballs* served in a marinara sauce.

Fans of Pizza is Lovely's pre-pandemic incarnation will find their Brewpub offering a little unfamiliar – for their signature Detroit-style you'll need to head to Renato's [p18]. At the Brewpub they have kept to the tried-and-tested approach that Mission Pizza had established, with a selection of interesting topping combinations across red and white bases – several of which can be served as gluten-free.

Alongside the food, Left Handed Giant's expansive bar offers a combination of LHG and guest beers from across the taste and style spectrum, usually with a decent number of beverages clearly labelled as vegan-friendly.

As well as its veggie/vegan Brewpub offering, Left Handed Giant also hosts a regular 'Vegan Fest' at its Taproom in St Philips, showcasing a generous smattering of vegan businesses including food and drink makers, creators and booksellers.

EAT IN DELIVERY

NADU

Destination for nourishing and vibrant Sri Lankan and Tamil cuisine

FLEXITARIAN

77-79 Stokes Croft, BS1 3RD

nadubristol.com

Nadu has quickly become known as one of Stokes Croft's most vibrant restaurants since it first opened in December 2020. On Friday and Saturday nights you can expect to walk into a cacophony of chatter from diners seated amidst a backdrop of retro Indian posters and traditional devil heads – a nod to the tales of *Ramayana*, a Sanskrit epic from ancient India.

Nadu draws on influences from both Sri Lanka and Tamil Nadu, the southernmost state of India. Executive chef Saravanan Nambirajan has worked in a number of Michelin-starred kitchens across the world; this is evident from the tastebud-enticing fare served at Nadu.

While the menu is omnivorous in nature, the vegan options truly shine. The hero dish has to be the *tear-and-share dosa* that arrives longer than your arm; equally, you won't want to pass up an opportunity to dive into one of the flavourful, rich curries. The *vambatu moju* – featuring aubergine and kokum – or the *kaju kari* – made with cashew nut, green peas and ground spices – are both delicious dishes that showcase delicacies from different regions in India, while a helping of sides including *sambar*, *masala potatoes* and *pickled mojo* mean that plant-based diners have plenty to choose from when ordering.

If you are planning to go on a weekend, you shold look to book well in advance to avoid disappointment. While you can order Nadu's menu for takeaway, it would be a shame to miss out on the colourful, dynamic buzz that you'll encounter when spending an evening in this delightful, lively venue.

YOU MUST TRY...

Vambatu Moju
Kaju Kari
Tear-and-Share Dosa

EAT IN TAKEAWAY DELIVERY

FOOD

17

CAFÉ KINO

Soulful, inclusive community-run vegan cafe-bar

VEGAN

108 Stokes Croft, BS1 3RU

cafekino.coop

Arguably Bristol's most socially-minded and progressive vegan joint, Café Kino has been around (in one form or another) since 1996. A workers non-profit co-operative – which runs as a collective – the Stokes Croft business reinvests any profit it makes straight back into improving the cafe.

Café Kino wasn't always a cafe; in the 90s it started out as a series of pop-up events hosted between Bristol and Cardiff, before morphing into a bricks-and-mortar hangout in its first premises on Ninetree Hill in 2006. In 2010 Café Kino relocated, opening in its current location and bringing fresh life to a space that had lain unoccupied for years.

You can expect simple but good grub done with a minimum of fuss: *mushrooms on toast, bean burgers, 'chkn' burgers, sausage rolls*, soups, salads and good old *BLTs*, as well as a burgeoning counter of cakes and pastries.

What is special about Café Kino is its commitment to working with local and independent businesses: using Essential Trading co-operative for its wholesale wholefoods and Four Seasons Organic for all of its fruit and veg needs.

Café Kino wears its heart on its sleeve and strives for inclusivity, aiming to be a safe and supportive place for all. The walls are adorned with artwork from local artists and the downstairs can be hired out affordably by local creatives looking to host events.

EAT IN TAKEAWAY

18

TUK TUCK

Budget- and belly-friendly pan-Asian fare

FLEXITARIAN

32 Stokes Croft, BS1 3QD • 5 St Stephen's Street, BS1 1EE

tuktuck.com

You go to some places to be wined and dined. Other places you go to for the pure love of the food it serves. One of those latter places is Tuk Tuck.

While each of its venues – one in the Centre and the other in Stokes Croft – serve up a slightly different menu, both offer pan-Asian fare that combine affordability with hunger-sating deliciousness, with dishes drawn from Korean, Japanese and Thai cusines, among others.

The menu might be geographically diverse but it isn't haphazard – each dish is a genuine crowd-pleaser inspired by the meals served up at street markets across Asia – from *bao buns* and dumplings to curries, *bibimbap* and croquettes.

One highlight across both venues is the *kimchi fries* – served with tofu, mushroom and spicy vegan mayo – while the *kimchi pancakes* (a popular Korean dish) are also worth trying out.

For the portion size and quality, Tuk Tuck is surprisingly affordable – allowing you to try a selection of sides and mains without breaking the bank.

Tuk Tuck isn't fully vegan but nearly every item on the menu comes with a vegan option (usually tofu or vegetable-based).

While the Stokes Croft venue is entirely indoors, the city centre location has outdoor seating overlooking the Cenotaph – a great place to relax on a summer's evening with a cold Asahi (or Cass) while munching your way through a portion of edamame.

For those who don't feel like wandering into the middle of town, never fear – Tuk Tuck is also available for delivery orders via Deliveroo.

YOU MUST TRY...

Kimchi Fries
Pumpkin Croquettes

EAT IN DELIVERY

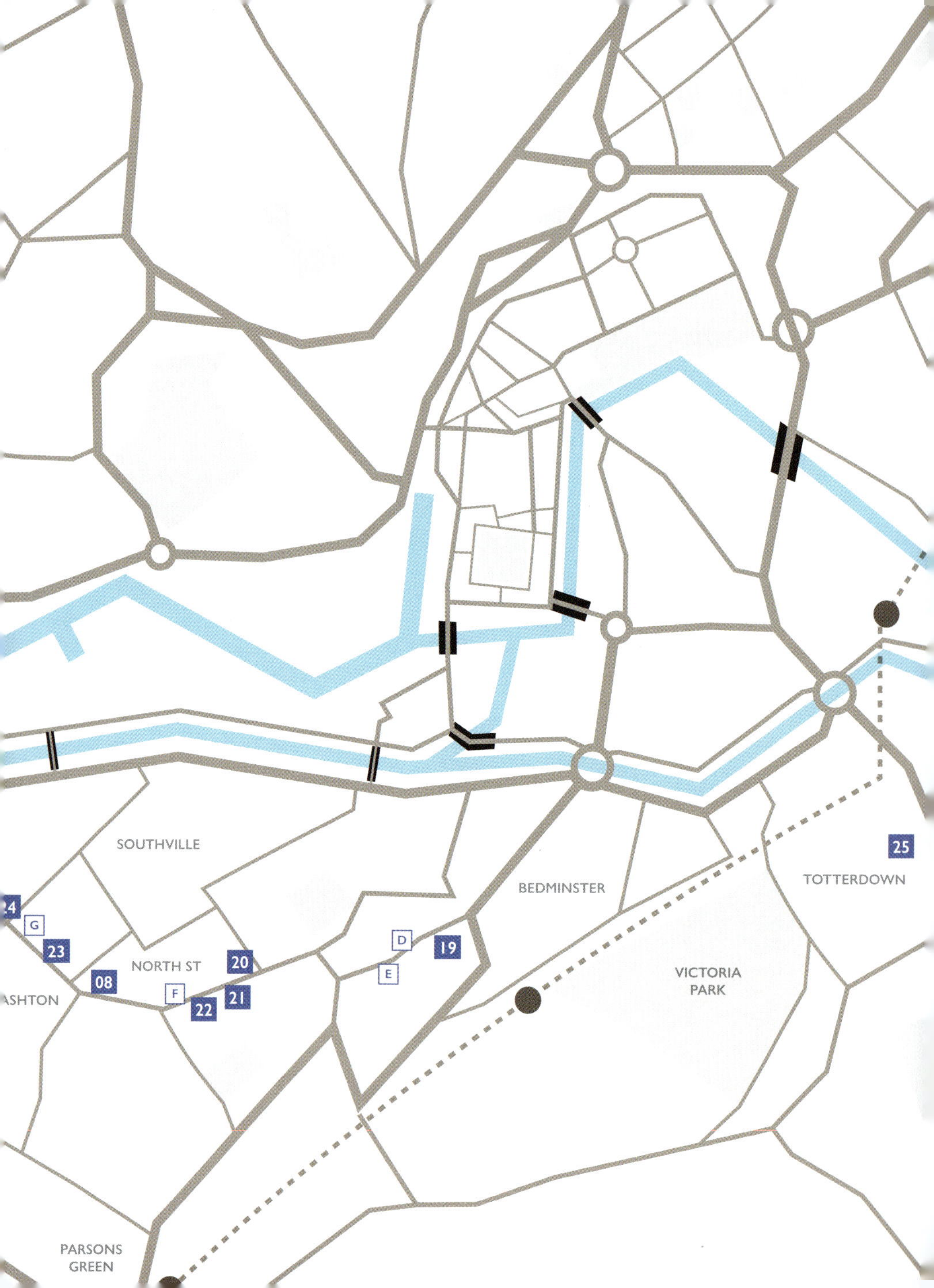
SOUTHVILLE
BEDMINSTER
TOTTERDOWN
25
24
G
23
NORTH ST
20
D
19
08
E
ASHTON
F
22
21
VICTORIA
PARK
PARSONS
GREEN

SOUTH BRISTOL

BS3 • BS4

THE BRISTOL LOAF

A bustling community hub serving bread, cakes and much more

FLEXITARIAN

96 Bedminster Parade, BS3 4HL • Beacon, Trenchard Street, BS1 5AR • 213 Church Road, Redfield, BS5 9HF

thebristolloaf.co.uk

It seems that The Bristol Loaf has been filled to the rafters since the moment it opened the doors to its Bedminster location back in September 2020. Situated just across from Bedminster Asda, The Bristol Loaf occupies a light, airy space that is constantly filled with a quiet hubbub as people queue for pastries and bread and sit chatting at the tables with a coffee or something more substantial.

Bendminster was Loaf's second site and acts as a central bakery for its venues. It still retains its original site in Redfield, where all of its patisserie is produced, as well as a third site at the newly renovated Bristol Beacon.

With bread forming a central part of its operations, it should come as no surprise that it also forms a large part of its seasonally changing brunch and lunch menus – including everpresent staples such as its homemade *sourdough crumpets.*

With a multi-cultural team of chefs at hand, The Bristol Loaf looks to craft a regularly updated menu with inspiration drawn from these diverse backgrounds and a strong focus on using fresh, in-season and locally sourced ingredients where possible.

While the menu is flexitarian, there is an emphasis on putting tasty, thought-provoking vegetarian and vegan options in the spotlight. At the time of writing the plant-based options on the menu include *roasted asparagus with seeded pesto* on focaccia, as well as an *onion bhaji and spiced potato salad.*

Meanwhile, their *hash browns* – served with one of Loaf's made-in-house sauces – almost deserve a category of their own as a standout side dish, or even as the main event if you're looking for a delicious stop-gap between meals.

The driving force behind The Bristol Loaf team is to create a space and experience that spans both the elevated and the everyday: somewhere you can pop in for a coffee and a loaf of bread one day and then treat your friends and family the next.

This type of 'one space for everyone' strategy can sometimes fall flat if venues take on more forms than they can manage; however, when you are as popular as The Bristol Loaf then the approach is validated. Just be warned that you may need to wait a bit if you turn up wanting a table during peak weekend hours.

EAT IN

ALBATROSS CAFÉ

Much loved pastel-hued hangout for coffee and cakes

VEGETARIAN • VEGAN

60 North Street, BS3 1HJ

@albatrosscafebristol

Running through the middle of Southville, North Street has undergone a huge transformation over the past decade – and perhaps nowhere exemplifies that shift better than Albatross Café.

Having taken on the lease of a derelict electrical store and persuaded the landlord to allow them to convert it into a café, Albatross founders Imogen and Louis have single-handedly transformed the space into a beautiful café. The light-filled space – complete with mismatched vintage furniture and dozens of plants – offers an excellent selection of coffees, pastries and larger bites.

Several of its pastries and cakes are vegan friendly, including croissants from Forest Bakery [p112] and a regularly rotating line-up of plant-based cakes from 404 Bakes [p100]. Coupled with a relaxed, friendly neighbourhood atmosphere and great quality coffee, Albatross has taken what was once a dilapidated, rundown retail unit and turned it into a genuine community asset for those living in Bedminster and coming in from further afield.

EAT IN   TAKEAWAY

THE OLD BOOKSHOP

European-inspired neighbourhood bar in the heart of North Street

VEGETARIAN • VEGAN

65 North Street, BS3 1ES

theoldbookshopbristol.com

It's a hard feat to create a locals' pub in the centre of a bustling city, but Laura and Neil – the powerhouse duo behind The Old Bookshop – have pulled it off. It is rare to pop in without seeing one or both of them chatting with customers, serving at the bar or enjoying a quiet drink. It's a venue that carries the right amount of rowdy on a weekend without ever becoming raucous.

The Old Bookshop offers a warren of cosy nooks, areas to perch at for a couple of drinks, and larger tables for bigger gatherings. With eight rotating keg options and three cask lines, their extensive range of German, Belgium and European beers always serves up something novel – and much of it is vegan friendly. They also serve a plentiful selection of natural wines, ciders, spirits and cocktails, including their famous Mezcals and Mules.

Having originally wanted to open a bar in Berlin before being thwarted by Brexit and the Covid-19 pandemic, Laura and Neil wanted The Old Bookshop to reflect their love for the sociable haunts found all over the German capital. They have clearly put their personal stamp on the venue, from the extensive German and Belgian bottle menu to the dozens of artworks supplied by local artists (a lot of them tattooists) that adorn the walls. The diverse music selection – heavily influenced by punk rock as well as showcasing local bands – also reflects their own tastes.

As vegans themselves, Laura and Neil wanted to replicate the accessibility of plant-based options that they'd experienced in Berlin in their own space. While the venue is no longer fully plant-based – a nod to the need for a locals' pub to attract a diverse clientele – the entire menu is vegetarian by default and each dish can be made vegan upon request.

The food line-up changes semi-regularly with an emphasis on dishes that pair well with beer. At the time of writing the kitchen serves a selection of *loaded fries* and *laffa wraps*; previous iterations have seen pub classics with a German twist (think sauerkraut, pretzels, currywurst and schnitzel burgers) and a Sunday Roast menu during the winter months.

You're likely to be drawn to The Old Bookshop for the extensive and carefully curated list of keg and cask beers – but stay for the emo playlist and neighbourly atmosphere. You won't be disappointed.

EAT IN

HELLES
LAGERBIER HELL

An intimate space for elevated small plates

FLEXITARIAN

81 North Street, BS3 1ES

correstaurant.com

Situated on the former site of the much-missed Flip Deli, COR has proven a delightful addition to North Street's bustling food culture, and has quickly become a go-to for a special night out. Hurry past on a winter night and see the warm glow of diners hunkered down in the windows feasting on an array of small plates; stroll past in the summer months to see diners basking in the window seats, soaking up the sun. Whether you are planning to stop somewhere for a long lunch with wine, treat your family for a special occasion or book in for a date night, COR is often the answer.

COR is a family-run business from husband and wife team, Mark and Karen Chapman: the restaurant is led by Mark, who spent his entire career in food and hospitality, training in fine dining for four years before working in six-star resorts in Sydney. Since moving to Bristol with Karen, he has spent the last six years as the Executive Chef at some of Bristol's favourite places to eat out: Bravas, Gambas, Cargo Cantina and Masa + Mezcal.

The vibe at COR is seasonal small plates, with the vegan menu driven by Head Chef, Victoria Colsell, who herself has thirteen years of experience in the industry.
The menu is updated almost daily based on what is inspiring the team, what ingredients are available seasonally and any existing items that can be incorporated into dishes – with a firm focus on sustainability and reducing waste where possible.

While the standard menu features meat, fish and dairy, a vegan menu is available for diners (as well as dairy-free, gluten-free and nut-free options). These change according to seasonality and availability with potential dishes including a delight of burnt shallot, wild garlic bucatini and roman-style artichoke.

As well as offering a thoughtful vegan menu, the COR team has invested in giving something back to the wider community, offering apprenticeships for young people through Bristol City and Weston colleges.

Despite being a newcomer on the scene, COR has already made waves in the culinary world. The restaurant has been awarded a *Bib Gourmand* by The Michelin Guide for the past two years, in 2023 and 2024, recognising its commitment to good quality, good value cooking. It's quite the recommendation.

EAT IN

Laid-back Middle Eastern-inspired cafe serving seriously good food all day

VEGETARIAN • VEGAN

238 North Street, BS3 1JD

yafo.co.uk

Some places feel the need to scream and shout about what makes them great. At Yafo they just let the food do the talking.

Launched on the site of a former butcher's in bustling North Street, since 2021 Yafo has delighted locals with rich Middle Eastern flavours done properly. In a full-throated commitment to authenticity, Yafo's chefs make all of the venue's hummus, falafel and other key ingredients in-house from scratch.

As well a superb *shuk* menu of wraps, pittas and salad boxes – perfect for a lunchtime meal – Yafo also offers a wide range of plates that put its signature hummus in the spotlight, including the *ful mudammas* (topped with crushed fava beans) and *hummus lahmeh* (featuring slow-cooked plant-based ragu and roasted pine nuts).

Having originally run with an evening menu of Middle Eastern-inspired small plates, Yafo has since updated its offering to include an all-day selection of larger plates. Among the highlights here is assuredly the 'From the Taboon' section, with a selection of authentic ingredients served on the eponymous Levantine flatbread that is traditionally baked in a taboon 'tandoor' clay oven.

The menu is unapologetic in staying true to its culinary roots; several dishes might have you grasping for your phones to look up unfamiliar terms as you try and figure out what *lachmagine* (a bit like a Syrian pizza), *matbucha* (tomatoes and bell peppers slow-cooked North African style) or *pilpelchuma* (a chili-garlic paste similar to hot sauce) might be.

Alongside a myriad of enticing mains (and a veggie/vegan burger selection to cater for all tastes), there are a number of sides that are worthy of attention, including the *pan-fried broccoli* served with dukkah and tahini, and moreish *crispy oyster mushroom wings* that'll have the table squabbling over who gets to have the last one.

In keeping with the relaxed and casual vibes, service is at the counter. As a small venue on North Street – it has a front and back patio, but not a huge number of tables – it can become busy at times, so booking ahead is advised for larger groups.

EAT IN

24

TOBACCO FACTORY CAFÉ-BAR

Amorphous, vibrant space that serves the whole community

VEGETARIAN • VEGAN

Raleigh Road, BS3 1TF

tobaccofactory.com

If North Street can be said to have a soul, then it surely resides in the Tobacco Factory. One of several repurposed former cigarette and cigar factory buildings south of the river, the Tobacco Factory building serves as home for an independent theatre, farm shop and, of course, the Tobacco Factory Café-Bar.

Spend any time here in this former public house and you'll be amazed how the space seems to shapeshift as the needs of its clientele change throughout the day.

Mornings see the place filled with laptop workers, casual meetings, and new parents meeting up with their young kids in tow. Where other places would be overwhelmed with such a range of visitors, Tobacco Factory's spacious ground floor layout – with floor-to-ceiling windows, an eclectic seating arrangement and semi-open kitchen – means it never feels cramped or rumbunctious as is the case with so many other venues.

In the evening the café-bar seamlessly adapts, welcoming drinkers and non-drinkers, board gamers, pub quizzers and even music lovers to its regular array of events. Weekends see Sunday brunch served until 3pm and a street market taking place just outside, both in the venue's yard and extending out onto Raleigh Road.

The food is without a doubt the underrated attraction at the Tobacco Factory. Drawing on the venue's links with Five Acre Farm and Mark's Bread (both owned by the same group), as well as the suppliers from its Sunday Markets, the venue offers a fully veggie/vegan selection of small plates, breakfast items and a smattering of mains and sides. Working with local suppliers means that menu items change regularly, with sustainability a key watchword. This extends to its coffee supplier, with B Corp-certified Clifton Coffee roasters chosen for their sustainable practices, as well as a commitment to using local breweries to supply nearly all of its entire range of alcoholic and non-alcoholic beverages.

Plant based highlights include its handmade *pie, mash and gravy* – with a 'Pie and Pint' deal running on Wednesdays – as well as its *soft corn tacos*. Those looking for something lighter to snack on, meanwhile, would be unwise to ignore the *grilled pitta with baba ganoush*, as well as the perfectly prepared pan-fried *padrón peppers*.

EAT IN

25

THE SUNDIAL KITCHEN

Thoughtful, homemade veggie dishes in a beautiful sunlit space

VEGETARIAN • VEGAN

1 William Street, BS3 4TU

thesundialkitchen.co.uk

The Sundial Kitchen was originally an events space on North Street (in what is now the Bristol Beer Factory Studio Bar) before the Covid pandemic forced it to close its doors. Given the opportunity to relocate to a recently refurbished building in Totterdown, husband-and-wife team Chloe and Paul opened the space initially as a shop-cum-takeaway operation due to the restrictions at the time – then opened fully as a restaurant and events space once these lifted.

Despite being tucked out of the way up a quiet street with little organic footfall (and only being open Friday to Monday at the time of writing), The Sundial Kitchen has managed to establish itself as a bit of a destination within its area, attracting locals and customers from across Bristol.

While the establishment is primarily a vegetarian one, they are keen to make sure that they provide ample options for vegan customers – as well as those who are gluten free. As much as possible is made from scratch by the team in-house: this includes the puff pastry, breads, cakes, kimchi and even the ferments they use. With this approach comes a commitment to seasonal and local produce, completely avoiding ingredients with considerable air miles such as avocado and tropical fruits.

The menu itself spans a few culinary genres and prides itself on offering unfussy, down-to-earth dishes that are also unexpected. This means you can expect to see typically British dishes – like the *big Sundial brunch* – rubbing shoulders with dishes drawn from Asian cooking (such as the *kimchi rice* and *Thai green curry*) or from across different European cuisines.

While the brunch menu largely remains consistent, the lunch menu is more of a moveable feast with items changing regularly – and usually feature at least one or two pasta dishes in a nod to chef Paul's expertise with Italian food.

As well as being open as a morning-to-afternoon food space, the two-floor venue doubles up as an evening events space for people wanting to host private community events – these have included weekly yoga classes, monthly comedy nights, several birthday parties and even the occasional wedding celebration.

EAT IN

26

CHEUNG'S VEGAN KITCHEN

Long-standing Chinese takeaway with a fully plant-based menu

VEGAN

89 St. Marks Road, BS5 6HY

cheungsvegankitchen.com

Takeaway restaurants don't normally make it into food guides. Then again, Cheung's is far from your average Chinese takeout.

First opened in 1969, Cheung's operated out of their Brislington location as a Chinese takeaway and a fish and chip shop for two generations, before completely shifting gears during the pandemic and becoming a darling of Bristol's vegan scene with an entirely plant-based menu of Chinese classics.

Denny and Linda – the husband-and-wife team that run Cheung's – had long wanted to offer vegan Chinese dishes, but had been held back by cross-contamination concerns. A decision to replace the fryer range gave them the opportunity to experiment and try something new, so they used this as an opportunity to test out a plant-based menu via Deliveroo. After seeing an overwhelmingly positive response to the switch they made the bold decision to abandon a planned return to fish and chips and meat dishes, instead reworking their menu to become a 100% vegan business.

The premise behind Cheung's menu is simple – to take the takeaway staples that had been most popular with their customers historically – such as *crispy chilli beef*, *kung po* and *chicken/pork balls* – and create an as-good vegan alternative that would be incredibly familiar taste-wise while offering a guilt-free eating experience.

This process involved cutting down their previous menu significantly – this had featured dozens of dishes including five different *chow meins* – and saw them focus instead on a simple selection of favourites that customers would easily recognise.

Extreme care has been taken to ensure that these dishes remain true to their meat-based predecessors; Denny and Linda even brought in a Michelin-recognised chef friend to assist with the design of the menu, matching their ambition to raise the bar on what people expect from a takeaway establishment.

While by their own admission Cheung's no longer gets as much passing trade from those living nearby, it has more than made up for it in delivery sales. It is not just likely to be the best vegan Chinese takeaway you've had, it might just be the best Chinese food you've ever eaten, period.

TAKEAWAY DELIVERY

I
REDLAND
H
C
THE
DOWNS
CLIFTON
DOWN
32
WHITELADIES
ROAD
THE
TRIANGLE
SUSPENSION
BRIDGE
27
28
29
31
30
CLIFTON
VILLAGE
BRANDON
HILL

WEST BRISTOL

BS8

27

KIBOU KITCHEN & BAR

Elegant Japanese dining with a large selection of vegan sushi, ramen and more

FLEXITARIAN

kibou.co.uk

16 King's Road, BS8 4AB

Some places feel like an experience as much as a meal. Kibou is one of them. With bold neon signage paired with traditional Japanese block prints, Japanese acers and dark wood panelled walls, Kibou feels like a well-balanced combination of old and new – mirrored by its diverse menu spanning sushi, noodles, ramen and bao.

Kibou means 'hope' in Japanese – if the name reflects founder Emma Graveney and her team's hopes that the restaurant could find a place in the hearts of diners, then they have little to worry about. Everything at Kibou is clearly done with love and appreciation for Japanese cuisine at its best.

While the menu is creative and varied, there is no ripping up of the rulebook or radical reinterpretation here: at its core Kibou promises to deliver the staples that you'd expect in a Japanese restaurant, and does this exceptionally well.

The vegan side of its menu delivers a selection of dishes that should please all palates, from its utterly sublime *nasu dengaku* – a charred half-aubergine falling off the skin and served with a delectable caramelised miso glaze – to its fresh and tastebud-tingling *yasai volcano rolls,* a ten-piece selection of tempura-fried futomaki filled with red pepper and avocado that deserves to be shared with others. That's without even mentioning the rich, warming *yasai ramen* with crispy tofu and fresh vegetables propped up in a delicious bath of noodles and a shiitake and miso broth.

Among the sides there are also some stand-out options. Try the *edamame* with black lava salt and you'll wonder why it isn't always served this way. Likewise the *dynamite cauliflower* and *kabocha korokke* (pumpkin croquettes) will earn rave reviews at most tables.

Alongside the food is a selection of sake, wine and both alcoholic and non-alcoholic cocktails – although you'll need to enquire as to which of these are suitable for vegans.

Alongside Kirin Ichiban on draught, Kibou also offers two vegan-friendly Hitachino Nest beers – a red rice ale and a Belgian-style white ale – which offers a novel experience for those keen to sample a more complex beer.

EAT IN

28

EDEN CAFÉ

Cosy vegan space in the heart of Clifton Village

VEGAN

edencafeclifton.co.uk

10 Waterloo Street, BS8 4BT

Trying to find a slice of quiet on a weekend in Clifton Village can be a challenge. Let us introduce you to Eden Café, a cosy vegan cafe tucked slightly off the beaten track on Waterloo Street. Eden Café is a fully vegan establishment that offers a smörgsbord of plant based meals, sweet treats and afternoon teas.

Eden Café's offering ranges from the healthy and pure – including a selection of stress-relieving and anti-imflammatory adaptogenic elixers – to sweet and indulgent cakes and donuts made by patisserie chef and owner Clara.

Accessibility and sustainability are core tenets that Eden Café takes seriously – the menu is designed to be soy-, nut- and gluten-free wherever possible, as well as avoiding less environmentally friendly ingredients such as avocado and almonds in their dishes. In keeping with this, their entire food menu is created in-house, including its vegan seitan and pastrami.

While it's not the biggest venue, there is a small amount of outdoor seating where you can people-watch from a quiet nook; the perfect place to kick back and relax away from the madding crowds.

EAT IN

29

EAST VILLAGE CAFÉ

An ever-popular haven of plant-based sweet and savoury delights

VEGAN

Boyce's Avenue, BS8 4AA

eastvillagecafe.co.uk

This famous Clifton Village vegan café is perennially heaving – and for good reason. East Village boasts perhaps the most extensive drinks menu you will ever come across: this includes everything from iced super lattes to coffees flavoured with lavender, strawberry, red velvet, or even rose and cardamom. There is also a decadent range of hot chocolate options that includes orange, vegan 'bueno', s'mores and pistachio. You're advised to give yourself a solid ten minutes before joining the queue to make your choice or forever risk a case of buyer's regret!

If you're in the mood for something savoury, East Village Café offers an all-day menu boasting seasonally changing soups, garlic and herb mushrooms on toast and various generously filled sandwiches and toasties.

The real culinary hero at East Village, however, is its abundant rotation of plant-based cakes and pastries. You can expect something a little different everyday, but regular highlights include the chocolate-covered chocolate croissants, s'mores brownies and banoffee cupcakes.

The café has a small seating area inside – often surrounded by a snake of customers queuing to order – along with a small shop in the back displaying jewellery, art, gifts and homewares from sister company French Grey.

During the warmer months you can enjoy the sunshine on the tables outside if you can find one free; alternatively, place your order to go and enjoy it on a bench in nearby Victoria Square.

You can expect to pay a premium for its prime location in the heart of Clifton Village: at the time of writing, sandwiches cost over £10 and smoothies come in at more than a fiver. Despite this, its burgeoning popularity is well deserved – even among the myriad coffee spots in Clifton, East Village Café stands out as a genuine gem of a place.

EAT IN TAKEAWAY

30

YAKINORI

No-fuss Japanese favourites for when you're on the go

FLEXITARIAN

78 Park Street, BS1 5LA

yakinori.co.uk

The kawaii-style illustrations covering every inch of wall space and the vibrant orange-and-green furniture might not be for everyone – yet Yakinori's relaxed, unpretentious and affordable menu more than makes up for its brightly decorated interior.

Vegan customers will be treated to an extensive menu that spans Yakinori's offering, from simple crowdpleasers like its *miso soup* and *yasai gyoza* to the highly recommended *teriyaki mushroom and miso aubergine bao bun*.

First-time visitors could do worse than sampling the *bento boxes* that Yakinori are best known for: the vegan version features pumpkin croquettes, firecracker cauliflower, miso aubergine, vegan sushi, pickles, slaw and sticky rice – and is served with a side of miso soup.

Yakinori might be fairly informal in style and uncomplicated in presentation – but it is a very well-priced option that delivers consistently good quality Japanese food with the minimum of fuss. That's no bad thing.

EAT IN TAKEAWAY DELIVERY

EATCHU

Delightful dumplings, rice boxes and noodles to go

FLEXITARIAN

1 Queens Row, Triangle, BS8 1EZ • Exchange Avenue, BS1 1JQ • City Business Park, St Jude's, BS5 0SP

eatchu.co.uk

Having started life serving out of the window at its miniscule site in St Nick's Market, Eatchu has quickly become known as a high water mark in terms of quality Asian food (in a city with plenty such options).

Eatchu serves a concise but belly-pleasing selection of Japanese specialities: these include its show-stopping *gyoza* (with both triple mushroom and broccoli, pea and edamame vegan options) as well as rice boxes that are far more delicious than they have any right to be – particularly the *Chef's Rice*, served with mayo, chilli oil, seaweed and red ginger.

Eatchu has expanded hugely across Bristol over the past year: as well as a temporary residency at the Wiper and True taproom in St Jude's and a food van often stationed at Wapping Wharf, the business has opened its second permanent space up the hill at the Triangle, offering a place for diners to stop and enjoy Eatchu's food on-site (the St Nick's site does have a couple of covered outdoor tables but is very much set up as a takeaway-first venue).

As well as being an ideal option for a quick delicious meal to take away, Eatchu is available on food delivery apps – so there's no excuse not to try it at least once. Your only regret is likely to be that you haven't gotten around to ordering it before.

YOU MUST TRY...

Chef's Rice
Curry Rice Box
Broccoli, Pea and Edamame dumplings.

EAT IN TAKEAWAY DELIVERY

32

NOT FOUND KITCHEN + 404 BAKES

Contemporary veg-led sharing plates and mouth-watering baked goods

VEGETARIAN • VEGAN

91A Whiteladies Road, BS8 2NT

@notfoundkitchen • @404.bakes

Anna, the culinary creator behind 404 Bakes, had no experience baking professionally to speak of when she first took on the responsibility of making cakes for what was then 404 Not Found, a popular café situated in a small site at the foot of St Michael's Hill.

Anna started out making a selection of smaller cakes and brownies (the cherry biscoff brownie gaining a cult following from those in the know), before expanding out into full-sized cakes as well. As the dessert selection at 404 Not Found grew, they soon discovered that there was wholesale demand for her creations, with her first client being New Cut Coffee on Whapping Wharf [p48].

It came to a point where the bakery side of the business had outgrown the Cotham premises and a decision was made to relocate to their current home on Whiteladies Road. It initially operated largely as a wholesale business but with a long-term pop up being operated in the front of the building by Roam Wild Coffee, which sold 404 Bakes alongside its drinks menu (and continues to do so from its roaming coffee van).

With the bakery still occupying the back of the building, the front has now been transformed into the Not Found Kitchen, a spiritual successor of the original venue that offers an eclectic and elevated – but reasonably priced – brunch and lunch menu of veggie/vegan sharing plates.

As well as a beautiful sun-lit café space, Anna and partner Chris have recently renovated the garden space to create a secluded sun trap for customers to enjoy.

It's taken a little while to get there but 404 Bakes and the Not Found Kitchen appear to have found their rightful home on Whiteladies Road.

Beyond their own space, you'll find 404 Bakes products in various locations across Bristol and the South West, including at Albatross Café [p68]. While their postal order online shop is closed at the time of writing, you can also order brownies for collection, as well as celebration and wedding cakes made to order.

EAT IN

D
C
42
41
ST ANDREWS PARK
THE ARCHES
40
J
MONTPELIER
38
C
ST WERBURGHS
STAPLETON ROAD
43
K
EASTON
37
08
39
35
ST PAULS
41
31
LAWRENCE HILL
G
D
34
33
OLD MARKET
36
ST PHILIP'S
TEMPLE MEADS

EAST BRISTOL

BS2 • BS5 • BS6 • BS7

CHIDO WEY

Bright and lively setting for relaxed Mexican food and cocktails

FLEXITARIAN

25B, Central Hall, Old Market, BS2 0HB

chidowey.co.uk

At Chido Wey, the only thing bolder and brighter than the colourful décor are the flavours themselves. The name – pronounced '*chee-doh way*' – translates as 'cool dude' in Mexican-Spanish slang, reflecting the team's ambition to bring a riot of Central American vibes to life in their corner of Old Market.

They have achieved this ambition with aplomb, with Latin-inspired murals daubed across the walls, an abundance of cacti and succulents and a broad flexitarian menu showcasing Cali-Mex classics. Even the smell when you come through the door – an enticing waft of toasted corn tortillas – takes you far away from the perenially grey skies of England.

Chido Wey's dishes draws on traditional elements – including the use of fruit sauces, typical Central American ingredients such as plantains and refried beans and liberal use of the classically Mexican spice *tajín*. These are taken and combined into the formats that British diners will be well familiar with – *burritos*, *tacos* and *quesdillas* are all available with a variety of fillings and flavours, along with *tostadas* and *nachos*.

With nearly half of the menu vegan-friendly, however, it's worth exploring off the beaten track a bit and trying something different, such as the *eloté* (grilled corn served with a spiced cream and coriander) or *pozole* (a vegetable and chilli broth made with maize kernels).

It would be remiss to ignore Chido Wey's cocktail menu: a selection of fruity, colourful (and occasionally spicy!) drinks along with Latin classics such as mojitos and capirinhas.

Importantly, considering the LGBTQ+ friendly vibe of Old Market, Chido Wey is deliberately set up as a queer-friendly establishment, with the team keen to create an environment that welcomes all. With its overwhelming sense of fun and playfulness, which can be felt across every dish they serve, it's hard not to like Chido Wey.

EAT IN

FI REAL

Authentic, healthy Caribbean fare made in a former bank

VEGAN

57 West Street, BS2 0BZ

fireal.co.uk

It is impossible to write about Bristol's food scene without acknowledging its wealth of Caribbean food, a legacy of the migrants from the West Indies invited to live and work in the UK during the 50s and 60s who ended up settling in Bristol and contributing to the city's culinary melting pot.

Among a rich tapestry of venues serving a variety of takes on this style of food (including Biblos [p40]), Fi Real offers its own authentic version of rich Jamaican cuisine that is well priced, richly appetising and entirely plant-based.

Operating out of the spacious site of a former bank building on West Street in Old Market, Fi Real prioritises serving healthy food with the punchy, deep flavours for which Caribbean cooking is deservedly known.

As well as veg-based classics such as *rice and peas*, *ital ackee* and *fried plantain*, Fi Real's menu also offers a number of plant-based takes on meatier options – its flavour-packed *jerk tofu and spicy kale* is a particular crowdpleaser, while a *Jamaican curry chunks* dish offers a soy-based take on Indo-Jamaican staple *curried goat*.

As well as its savoury menu, Fi Real offers a selection of plant-based desserts, including its much-loved *Jamaican banana cake*. It also offers a selection of homemade fresh fruit drinks, soft drinks and non-alcoholic beverages.

In addition to serving diners at its West Street premises, Fi Real also accepts takeaway orders and has a slightly more limited, but still delicious, menu for those wanting to order for delivery.

It is worth noting that the establishment has slightly unusual operating hours, being closed on Fridays and Saturdays but then open the rest of the week.

EAT IN TAKEAWAY DELIVERY

35

BABA GANOUSH KITCHEN

Bright, vibrant venue for affordable Middle Eastern food

VEGAN

81 St Nicholas' Road, BS2 9JJ

@babaganoushkitchen

Even if you've not been to Baba Ganoush Kitchen, the chances are that you'll have spotted it. Situated just off the start of the M32 on St Nicholas' Road, it is an explosion of colour and positive vibes both inside and out. It exterior is certain to grab your attention – not least its sign claiming to offer the 'World's Best Wrap'.

Whether it is literally world-beating is another discussion entirely but there is no doubt that its *baba wraps* are worth the pilgrimage. Available in two vegan options – falafel or cauliflower, potato and aubergine – they are filled to bursting with salad, pickles, tahini and chilli sauce, these generously sized servings feel an absolute steal at £6 apiece.

Beyond wraps, Baba Ganoush offers two combo *vegan mezze* plates, as well as a selection of individual mezze items, including *dolmados* (stuffed vine leaves), *kaushari* (rice and lentils topped with tahini, chilli and crispy onions) and its eponymous *baba ganoush*.

YOU MUST TRY...

Falafel Baba Wrap
Beirut Vegan Mezze

EAT IN TAKEAWAY

36

FOREST BAKERY

Moreish plant-based pastries baked in a Bristolian railway arch

VEGETARIAN • VEGAN

Arch 7, Silverthorne Lane, BS2 0QD

theforestbakery.co.uk

It might seem strange to have a working bakery, which only sells a few items out of a railway arch tucked down a side road, in a vegan food guide. However, anyone who has tried Forest Bakery's pastries will know exactly why we've included it.

The bakery was founded by Jimmy, a former art teacher who gave up his career to work for an artisan bakery in Somerset, learning the art of quality patisserie for a number of years before moving to Bristol to start his own business.

Originally conceived as a mix of retail and wholesale, the burgeoning business reached a critical point when the pandemic struck, with a switch over to an online, delivery-based model which became the route to success. Nowadays the business is mostly wholesale, having built up its clientele from a couple of cafés – including Fox & West – to a whole raft of businesses across Bristol (including some of the businesses featured in this guide).

While vegan pastries were always part of the business model they now make up 95% of the bakery's offering, with plant-based pastries in high demand due to being accessible to a wider range of customers.

One advantage of this is cost – recent price rises mean cow's butter is now nearly twice the price of a quality vegan alternative, so Forest Bakery can be competitive with suppliers that use dairy in their products.

The bakery itself produces a limited menu of quality items rather than trying to do it all – with classics such as *pain au chocolate* offered alongside *pistachio swirls, almond croissants, focaccia* and *pain au raisin.*

This focus on doing things well and using quality ingredients is key to Forest Bakery's popularity among Bristolian venues. While increasingly popular, Jimmy has no plans to expand the business beyond Bristol.

Instead, Forest Bakery straddles that happy line of being 'big enough to cope but small enough to care'. It's an ethos that is palpable in every delicious bite.

TAKEAWAY

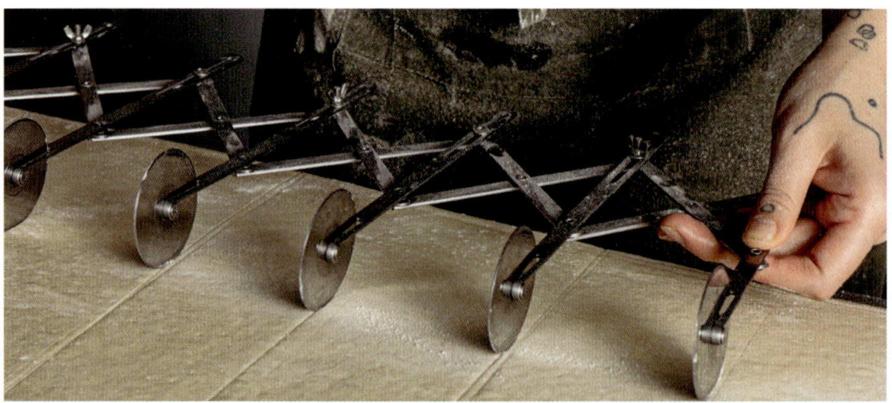

37

THALI MONTPELIER

Thali curries and tiffin takeaways made to family recipes

FLEXITARIAN

12 York Road, BS6 5QE

thalirestaurant.co.uk

The story goes that Thali Restaurant began life as a street food truck at Glastonbury Festival after founder Jim Pizer travelled to India and fell in love with the food. Fast forward to 2024 and the Thali Restaurant Montpelier – just a bit further down the road from The Bristolian [p121] and Oowee's Picton Street site [p32] – operates as a love letter to Indian cusine, drawing inspiration from across the subcontinent.

The Thali team is headed by a female chef, Asha, who uses many of the family recipes that were handed down to her and a smattering of dishes from her family's restaurant in rural India – this includes the downright delicious and highly recommended *masala-fried potatoes*.

Vegan, gluten-free and vegetarian options feature prominently on the menu, with three separate plant-based thalis and nearly all the sides and snacks being suitable for vegan diners.

As well as more familiar options such as Cobra, Thali also offers Roar beer – a vegan Asian-inspired lager whose profits go partly towards providing training for workers in the hospitality sector.

The restaurant itself is casual and relaxed, plastered with old school Bollywood posters and has bright colourful walls that reflect the vibrancy of the dishes.

As well as its spacious restaurant – making it a good option for larger groups – Thali offers an 'eco-friendly' tiffin takeaway, where customers can order an insulated tiffin tin filled with a thali of their choice.

YOU MUST TRY...

Pumpkin Olan Thali
City Snacks (Aloo Bonda, Samosa, Pakoda)
Masala-fried Potatoes

EAT IN TAKEAWAY

ROAR
PREMIUM CRAFT BEER

ROAR
PREMIUM CRAFT BE

KOOCHA MEZZE BAR

Persian and Middle Eastern establishment serving plant-based mezze

VEGAN

203B Cheltenham Rd, BS6 5QX

koochamezzebar.com

Having been vegan since it opened, Koocha has always set out to do things a bit differently from the norm. This is reflected in a 100% plant-based Middle Eastern menu with heavy Persian influences that is unafraid to take risks and play with unusual but delicious ingredient combinations.

Cases in point are the *parmesan sprouts*, served with turmeric, chopped chestnuts and a cumin yoghurt, and the *doner bao buns*, which pair the fluffy white steamed buns with a kebab-like shaved seitan filling, hoisin sauce and a chilli and mint sauce.

While these experimental dishes add a layer of additional intrigue to proceedings, it is the Persian and Middle Eastern staples that really show Koocha's class. Its *tzatziki* is a refreshing, light and lemony dish packing enough garlic to linger on your tongue untill you arrive home; while its *artichoke dip* with basil and walnuts is a real show stopper. Both deserve to be ordered along with a portion of *za'atar flatbread* to soak up all the delicious flaovurs.

Another highlight worth considering is the *ghormeh sabzi* – a deeply satisfying Persian stew with kidney beans and saffron rice. In what might be an unexpected turn, Koocha is also known for its vegan Sunday roasts where familiar British elements are given a unique Middle Eastern twist.

Koocha had skittered between locations in and around the Arches before it settled on its current location on Cheltenham Road. Its site is now unmissable: a bright blue frontage adorned with street art of white flowers and surly cheetahs. Inside you'll find a calming splash of stylised blues and yellows and a pleasantly humming sense of business as tables fill and empty throughout the evening.

EAT IN TAKEAWAY

39

THE BRISTOLIAN

Vibrant flexitarian café known for its breakfasts

FLEXITARIAN

2 Picton Street, Montpelier, BS6 5QA

thebristolian.co.uk

With its foliage-covered exterior and interior, there are obvious comparisons to its sister site Garden of Easton [p134], but The Bristolian's slimmed-down menu is definitely focused more on crowd-pleasing classics that all can enjoy. For plant-based customers, this includes a *vegan burger* made with jackfruit, tempeh, black beans and beetroot, as well as a mixed-vegetable *vegan quesadilla*.

Brunch is where this venue really shines. The Bristolian has a deserved reputation as one of the city's premier institutions for mid-morning dining, with its generously-sized fried breakfasts – including a fully vegan option featuring scrambled tofu, sesame-infused spinach and crispy aubergine – a real menu highlight.

The venue is walk-in only and its popularity means it can be difficult to get a table at weekends; however, takeaway options are available for those who are unable to find a seat when it gets busy.

EAT IN TAKEAWAY

KAL DOSA

Fiery Southern Indian delights and crispy dosas

FLEXITARIAN

16, The Promenade, Gloucester Road, BS7 8AE

kaldosa.co.uk

It's obvious from the moment you walk through the door that Kal Dosa sits in the Nutmeg and Nadu family of restaurants – from the Indian matchbox artwork adorning the walls to the happy splashes of pastel pink and green lining the interiors.

Opened by Raja Munuswamy and Saravanan Nambirajan (the team behind Nadu) as well as Jyoti Patra, the concept behind Kal Dosa aims to take you on a culinary train ride through the four states that make up Southern India: Tamil Nadu, Kerala, Andhra Pradesh and Karnataka.

Inspired by their own adventures on the Southern Indian railways, the three owners wanted to highlight how train stations in South India are not just functional as we know them to be in the UK, but also serve as culinary havens. Over there, you can step off a train and be faced with a riot of delicious smells from stalls and restaurants all vying for your attention with their servings of local specialties.

While Kal Dosa is set up as an omnivorous restaurant, the cuisine of South India lends itself naturally to veg-centric dishes. If you're overwhelmed by choice, opt for the *vegan thali* (served at lunchtimes from Thursday to Sunday). This is made up of a selection of dishes served on a platter so you can nibble on a bit of everything.

As the name might suggest, however, Kal Dosa is most famous for its huge sharing *dosas*: savoury style pancakes made from soaked lentils and rice served with sambar and chutneys. They have five different styles of dosa on their menu, with three of them suitable for vegans.

Be warned, a lot of the menu at Kal Dosa is on the spicy side – so if you're not too keen on heat you might want to check with staff about the spice level of your dish before ordering.

YOU MUST TRY...

Gutti Venkaya Koora (slow-roasted aubergine in a peanut sauce)
Mysore Masala Dosa

EAT IN DELIVERY

ROSE BRAND
SAFETY MATCHES
INDIAN ANTELOPE
MATCHES
MADE IN INDIA

41

REAL HABESHA

Authentic, soulful and hearty Ethiopian and Eritrean food from a father-daughter duo

FLEXITARIAN

163 Gloucester Road, BS7 8BE • 146 Stapleton Road, BS5 0PU

realhabesha.com

Temesgen Tekie opened Real Habesha five years ago with the help of his daughter Freselam; in that time they've built an iconic space for Ethiopian and Eritrean food which boasts a loyal, local following.

Their first location on Stapleton Road is a real '*If you know, you know*' joint: a totally unfussy, practical establishment heaving with regulars who know to look beyond the economical interior and focus on the amazing smells and tastes of the food being served.

Habesha's second site on Gloucester Road opened in 2023 and offers more of a slice of East Africa. Splashes of red and yellow adorn the walls alongside murals depicting traditional Ethiopian scenes of families and friends sharing meals together. Some of the serving tables are of the traditional hand-weaved Ethiopian/Eritrean style: the perfect size to lay out a portion of *injera* covered with East African delicacies.

Both restaurants serve the same hearty, delicious family-inspired dishes from Ethiopia and Eritrea; while the restaurant is flexitarian, the vegan sharing platter is incredible and the portion sizes on the generous side.

While the style of cuisine might be unfamiliar to some, don't let that put you off; all of the component ingredients in Habesha's dishes will be familiar to western palates. Sit down to a *combination dish* of cabbage, potatoes, carrot, green beans, red lentil curry with turmeric, kale, tomatoes, onions and shiro (ground chickpea stew) served alongside plenty of *injera* – the fermented flatbread that everything is served upon.

It's the epitome of comfort food – tasty, warming and filling – with generous portion sizes, it is guaranteed that you won't go hungry. As is typical with Ethiopian and Eritrean cuisine, the food is designed to be eaten with your hands so tear off a strip of *injera* and use it to grab whatever on the plate takes your fancy.

To finish it off, order their show-stopping coffee made using Ethiopian Sidamo beans. You'll leave happily sated – and wondering how soon is too soon to return.

EAT IN TAKEAWAY DELIVERY

42

VEGAN INDIA

Familiar British-Indian dishes served using plant-based alternatives

VEGAN

189 Gloucester Road, BS7 8BG

vegan-india.co.uk

For those of us who have been vegan for a while and have been conditioned to slender plant-based pickings, being presented with an abundence of choice can be a strangely alarming experience.

Step inside the neon green and pink oasis of Vegan India on Gloucester Road with its wildly extensive offering of 100% vegan options and you'll likely have a hearty dose of decision fatigue – in a good way – before you've finished browsing the menu.

If you've been sticking to *sag aloo* and *tadka dal* as the only safe plant-based options at your local Indian, you're in for a welcome treat: Vegan India's menu is chock full of the likes of mock *lamb biryani, vegan butter 'chicken'* or *'lamb' tikka masala.*

Vegan India certainly know how to play to a crowd, serving the traditional dishes you'd find at British-Indian restaurants all over the country – think *kormas, bhunas, jalfrezis, vindaloos, dansaks* and more – each with the choice of vegetables, tofu, or vegan versions of chicken, lamb, shrimp, meatball or tempeh.

A selection of specials exists to entice more adventurous palates, showcasing some less well known curries. These include *Korai, Achari, Makhani* (complete with vegan cheese) and even a butternut squash-based *Koda* curry.

One key unfulfilled craving for vegans at Indian restaurants is a buttery naan – there is no such worry here. Order from *plain, garlic, peshwari, keema* or *bahari* naans.

The vibe in Vegan India is unfussy and relaxed; the food, meanwhile, is spectacular. With Cobra on tap (and an extensive non-alcoholic menu), poppadoms with vegan sundries and delicious flavours abounding. It's everything you might want from a local Indian – but completely vegan to boot.

You can also order Vegan India's menu for delivery – making it an ideal option whether you're looking for a night out on the town or just wanting to relax on the sofa at home.

EAT IN | TAKEAWAY | DELIVERY

HALF
PINT
UK
CA
CE
M23
M23
0071

43

GARDEN OF EASTON

Plant-filled restaurant with a North African aesthetic and plates that pack a punch

FLEXITARIAN

89 St. Marks Road, BS5 6HY

thegardenofeaston.co.uk

You don't expect to come across a bona fide jungle in the middle of Easton – but it's a welcome surprise. This foliage-filled destination bathed in light is the brainchild of the same team behind the well-regarded breakfast favourite The Bristolian [p121] – and it is quickly apparent that they have poured their heart and soul into their Easton-based project.

Based over two floors with rustic wood furniture to accompany the menagerie of greenery, the venue was transformed by James, Ollie and Emma after they took it on in 2019 – remodelling and metamorphosing the whole space while keeping a nod to the venue's past as a veggie/vegan restaurant.

While the menu does offer a couple of meat and dairy options, the vast majority of the menu remains plant-focused with vegetables considered the centrepiece of each of the dishes they serve.

Even in winter, this venue feels far closer to Marrakesh than inner-city Bristol – this feeling of being somewhere beyond Bristol is accentuated by the sheer amount of plant life in the venue, which requires the staff to spend up to three hours watering each day in the height of summer.

'Nourishment' is the watchword of the Garden of Easton's food: strong flavours and bold, bright colours evident throughout the menu, from its rich and punchy *pistachio hummus* (the winner of a hummus-making competition among the staff) to its vibrant *cabbage salad*, which comes with a piquant vegan cashew pesto.

The venue offers different menus to suit different times of day, with a brunch-focused offering during the day including a vegan or veggie breakfast and tostadas.

The evening menu, meanwhile is dedicated to a range of robust, filling small plates. Among these are a majestic *sticky crispy aubergine* dish with grilled green pepper and kecap manis and perhaps the most unexpected delight on the menu: *artichoke hearts* on a bed of exquisite whipped miso tofu with charred spring onions, crispy capers and sorrel.

In addition to its plentiful number of plant-based options, the venue's house wine is always vegan-friendly and there is a generous range of hot drinks, cocktails and mocktails on offer.

EAT IN

ESTE KITCHEN

Small Latin American-inspired cafe off the beaten track

FLEXITARIAN

7 Greenbank Road, Greenbank, BS5 6EZ

estekitchen.com

Tucked in among the terraces of Greenbank, Este Kitchen is a small-but-sweet community focused café that offers an unexpectedly wide ranging selection of vegan-friendly dishes inspired by Latin American cuisine.

Este's motto is '*hecho con amore*' – made with love – and this is evident in their efforts to bring authentic Latin American ingredients to the table, with *patacones* (fried plantains), *frijoles* (black beans) and *cassava* (a South American staple) all present on a diverse menu.

Este's vegetarian and plant-based options range from a Latin-inspired Vegan Breakfast to various *arepas*, *empanadas*, *rice bowls* and even *plantain chips* served with guacamole. While the style of food served lends itself well to being veganised, it is a rare but welcome sight to see a small local venue make a concerted effort to provide such a varied offering for plant-based consumers.

As well as its food menu, Este offers a range of hot and cold drinks (including Columbian '*refrescos*'), a vegan-friendly smoothie menu and a small selection of cakes (often featuring one or two plant-based options).

The venue is definitely on the small side – with only a few tables in the café itself and a couple more on the wooden decking outside – which means that Este Kitchen fills up quickly, particularly at weekends. It's not a place to visit if you are in a hurry to get served, although they do offer a takeaway service if you find yourself short of time.

YOU MUST TRY...

Vegan Breakfast
Bandeja Paisa (sharing platter)
Empanadas (with Banana Blossom)

EAT IN TAKEAWAY

VEGAN PROVISIONS

BS1 • BS2 • BS3 • BS5 • BS6 • BS7 • BS8 • BS9

A THE HAPPY COW

@the_happy_icecream_van

Narrow Quay, Harbourside, BS1

Claiming to serve the UK's first plant-based whippy ice cream, The Happy Cow has established itself in recent years as a fixture along Narrow Quay – a stone's throw from the centre and located directly opposite the bars and restaurants of the Waterfront.

Happy Cow's ice cream is made with plant-based milk and coconut oil; it's served in a nostalgic 'Mr Whippy' style, which can be accompanied by a range of plant-based waffle cones, sauces and other toppings.

B HERBIVORE

herbivore-vegan-deli.co.uk

Unit 4, Cargo 2, Wapping Wharf, BS1 6ZA

It's certainly Bristol's smallest vegan deli – but it's also one of its mightiest. This family-run independent deli is tucked into a half-sized shipping container along Wapping Wharf's main drag.

Herbivore serves as the perfect pit stop if you're in the market for sourdough toasties, salad bowls, sumptuous cakes and other plant-based snacks.

Alternatively, pick up some of their other vegan goodies, such as its range of home-made preserves or its wide range of plant-based cheeses – including those from local supplier Kinda Co.

C C C BETTER FOOD

betterfood.co.uk

1-5 Gaol Ferry Steps, Wapping Wharf, BS1 6WE • 94A Whiteladies Road, Clifton, BS8 2QX • 21 Sevier Street, St Werburghs, BS2 9LB • 278 Gloucester Road, Horfield, BS7 8PD

Better Food is a local chain of ethical and sustainable stores with locations in Wapping Wharf, St. Werburghs, Whiteladies Road and Gloucester Road.

Each store also boasts a small cafe area with a deli counter where you can stop by solo with a book or pick up a snack to take away with you for later.

Organic, *local* and *ethical* are the founding principles at Better Food and the stores stock a mixture of fresh fruit and veg, snacks, chilled items like tofu, dips, vegan cheeses as well as ethical cleaning, household and beauty items.

D D D PRESERVE

preservefoods.co.uk

72 East Street, Bedminster BS3 4EY • 208 Gloucester Road, Bishopston BS7 8NU • 132 Church Road, Redfield, BS5 9HH • 71 Westbury Hill, Westbury on Trym, BS9 3AD

Having first opened in Gloucester Road, Preserve Foods now operates four stores across the city selling zero waste and packaging-free food and drink items – including pourable dried foods, herbs and spices, tea and coffee and even nut butters – alongside a selection of plastic-free household goods.

As well as its physical locations, Preserve operates a comprehensive 'click-and-collect' service, allowing customers to select the items they need online, then designate which of their four premises they wish to collect them from.

E VX

vxbristol.com

123 East Street, Bedminster, BS3 4ER

Vx is reminiscent of the pioneering vegan scene of 2015 – no frills, no fuss, and offering a one-stop-shop for niche vegan shopping needs. Run out of nutritional yeast? Need some vegan yorkshires or a centrepiece for your plant-based Sunday roast? Whatever you need, the chances are that Vx stocks it.

Together with its well-provisioned store, Vx runs a café focused on sweet-tooth tempting desserts – including giant slabs of *oreo blondie* – and a menu of food seemingly designed as the perfect hangover cure. This includes the carb-fest *mac and cheese burrito* and an extra fiery *hell burger*.

F ZERO GREEN

zerogreenbristol.co.uk

80 North Street, Southville, BS3 1HJ

A presence on North Street since 2018, Zero Green is currently run by Rob and Arwen, who took over the business when founders Lidia and Stacey decided it was time to move on.

Zero Green has a local-first mindset and offers a wide stock of frozen items, cleaning and household goods and both packaging- and plastic-free groceries.

As well as an online shop boasting thousands of items, Zero Green also operates a 'container library' of jars donated by other customers – handy if you forget to bring your own!

G G SOUTHVILLE DELI

southvilledeli.com

262 North Street, BS3 1JA • 259-261 Church Road, BS5 9HT

Primarily a wholefoods store with shops on both North Street and Church Rd, Redfield, Southville Deli also has a deli and hot drinks counter at both of its site – as well as plentifully-stocked chilled and frozen sections.

Southville Deli is the perfect place to stop by if you are in the market for fancy chocolates like Bouja Bouja, or to grab a delicious freshly-made sandwich to go, or to stock up on nuts, seeds and legumes from its packaging-free section. It also has a varying but generally available selection of plant-based meat alternatives.

H SCOOP WHOLEFOODS

scoopwholefoods.com

98A Whiteladies Road, Clifton, BS8 2QY

Claiming to be 'the UK's largest range of natural and organic wholefoods in bulk', Scoop operates stores in Bristol and Bath, as well as an online store with both collection and nationwide delivery.

Scoop works with its suppliers to ensure that its products are provided in reusable or compostable packaging, which can then be collected, sterilised and refilled with new products.

While the store isn't completely plant based, it does offer a decent range of clearly labelled vegan-friendly ingredients and produce.

I WILD OATS

woats.co.uk

9-11 Lower Redland Road, Redland, BS6 6TB

Bristol's oldest health and wellbeing store, Wild Oats, opened in 1981 and remains as vibrant and busy as ever.

As you step inside you are greeted to a veritable haven of baked goods and lattes at the counter, a chilled and frozen section with meat and cheese alternatives and a hoard of vitamins, supplements, eco-friendly household essentials and beauty products.

Wild Oats also hosts regular events and loyalty days, as well as co-organising the Lower Redland Road Market with nearby business The Bristol Artisan.

J HARVEST

harvest-bristol.coop

11 Gloucester Road, Bishopston, BS7 8AA

A vegan and vegetarian health and wholefood shop that is part of the Essential worker cooperative, Harvest serves up a sizeable zero waste selection (both food and household items) and fresh fruit and vegetables, as well as a deli counter serving a variety of savoury and sweet snacks, cakes and rolls – more than half of which are vegan friendly.

Being part of a cooperative, Harvest's emphasis is on fairly traded, organic and environmentally friendly goods. Its zero waste approach means it operates a 'no carrier bags' policy, instead offering sustainable alternatives in-store.

K MATTER WHOLEFOODS

matterwholefoods.uk

1 Greenbank Road, Greenbank, BS5 6EZ

Just up the road from Este Kitchen [p138], Matter Wholefoods is a family-run store offering organic and locally sourced fruit and vegetables, fresh bread from the Assembley Bakery in Old Market, a decent selection of vegan meat and plant milk alternatives and even a weekly subscription service for various products – including a veg box, a vegan meat box and a whole foods box.

Orders placed via Matter Wholefood's website are delivered via electric van and the space itself plays host to a regular line-up of events, supper clubs, workshops and talks.

ACKNOWLEDGEMENTS

We'd like to thank all of the brilliant restauranteurs, chefs and staff who allowed us to come and interview them for the book, sample their amazing food and photograph their menus: Gal at **Yafo** (who was our first interviewee!), Raja and Saravanan of **Nutmeg** and **Nadu** (and Jyoti from **Kal Dosa**); Prabha and the staff at **Dhamaka**, Lina at **Oowee**, Amy and Tam from **Ahh Toots**, Will at **Biblos**, Rob at **Root**, Tom at **Seven Lucky Gods**, Laura and Neil at **The Old Bookshop**, Lucy at **The Bristol Loaf**, Mark and Karen at **COR**, Molly and the **Tobacco Factory Café-Bar** team, Chloe and Paul at **Sundial Kitchen**, Denny and Linda at **Cheung's**, Paige at **Eden Café**, Anna at **404 Bakes** and the **Not Found Kitchen**, Conor at **Chido Wey**, Jimmy and the **Forest Bakery** team, Rajni and Asha at **Thali Montpelier**, Anna of **Garden of Easton** and **The Bristolian** and, last but by no means least, Freselam and Temesgan of **Habesha**.

We'd also like to take a beat to recognise some of the amazing businesses that we had intended to feature but announced they were having to cease operations before the book could be published – particular mention goes to the wonderful teams at **Mission Pizza** and **Future Doughnuts** who gave up their time to be interviewed by us. Your presence is sorely missed.

Thanks to Rob McCabe for your time and patience in proofing the book and spotting more mistakes that we'd care to admit!

Finally, a thanks to Joe Burt and the **Bristol Books** team for choosing to work with us as we sought to bring *Vegan Bristol* to a wider audience, as well as **Essential**, who kindly agreed to sponsor the book and help us to bring this idea to life. We are eternally grateful to you all.

Helena and Ben

PROUDLY SPONSORED BY

Essential

@EssentialTrading

www.essential-trading.coop

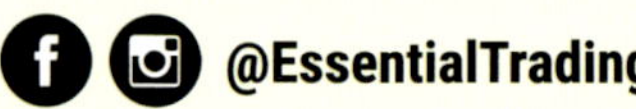

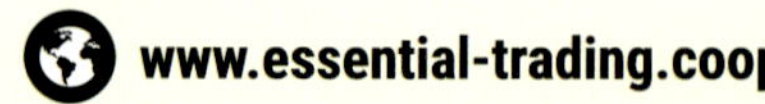

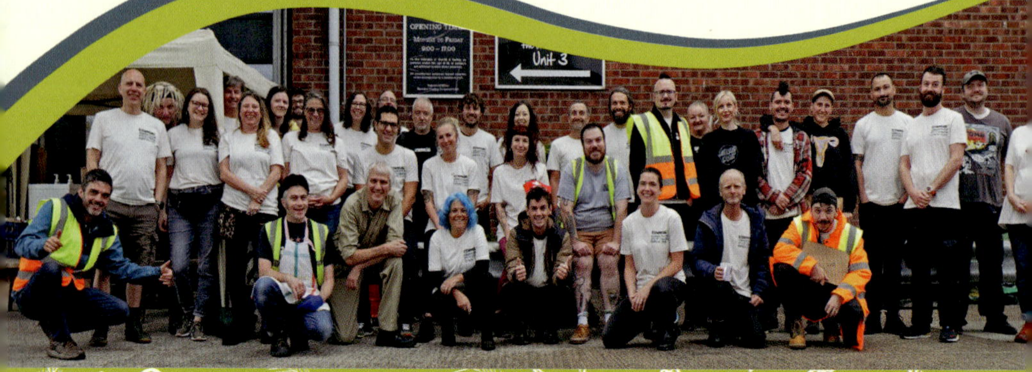

At Essential, we believe that ethical business practices and sustainable living go hand in hand. As a Bristol-based worker cooperative, we are passionate about providing high-quality, ethically sourced products to our customers while promoting environmental stewardship and social responsibility.

With roots going back to 1971, Essential has always been dedicated to supporting independent farmers, artisans, and producers who share our values. We prioritise fair trade relationships, ensuring that everyone involved in the production process is treated with dignity and respect.

Our extensive range of vegan and vegetarian products includes organic foods, cruelty-free body care items, eco-friendly household goods, and much more. From delicious plant-based snacks to nourishing skincare solutions, each item is carefully selected to meet our rigorous standards for quality and sustainability.

As a cooperative, we operate on principles of democracy, equality, and solidarity. By choosing Essential products, you are not only supporting a local business but also joining a movement toward a more just and compassionate world.

Together, we can make a difference, one ethical purchase at a time.